D1451552

BOMB SQUAD
TECHNICIAN

BY NICK GORDON

Are you ready to take it to the extreme?
Torque books thrust you into the action-packed world
of sports, vehicles, mystery, and adventure. These books
may include dirt, smoke, fire, and dangerous stunts.
WARNING: read at your own risk.

Library of Congress Cataloging-in-Publication Data

Gordon, Nick.
Bomb squad technician / by Nick Gordon.
    p. cm. -- (Torque : dangerous jobs)
Includes bibliographical references and index.
Summary: "Engaging images accompany information about bomb squad technicians. The combination
of high-interest subject matter and light text is intended for students in grades 3 through 7"--Provided by
publisher.
ISBN 978-1-60014-777-7 (hardcover : alk. paper)
1. Bomb squads--Juvenile literature. 2. Explosives--Juvenile literature. I. Title.
HV8080.B65G67 2013
363.17'98--dc23   2012002398

This edition first published in 2013 by Bellwether Media, Inc.

Printed in the United States of America, North Mankato, MN.

TABLE OF CONTENTS

CHAPTER 1

IT'S A BOMB!

The phone rings at the police station. Someone has found a suspicious backpack at the airport. The bomb squad rushes into action. They race to the scene as people **evacuate**. The technician puts on a protective suit and goes inside.

5

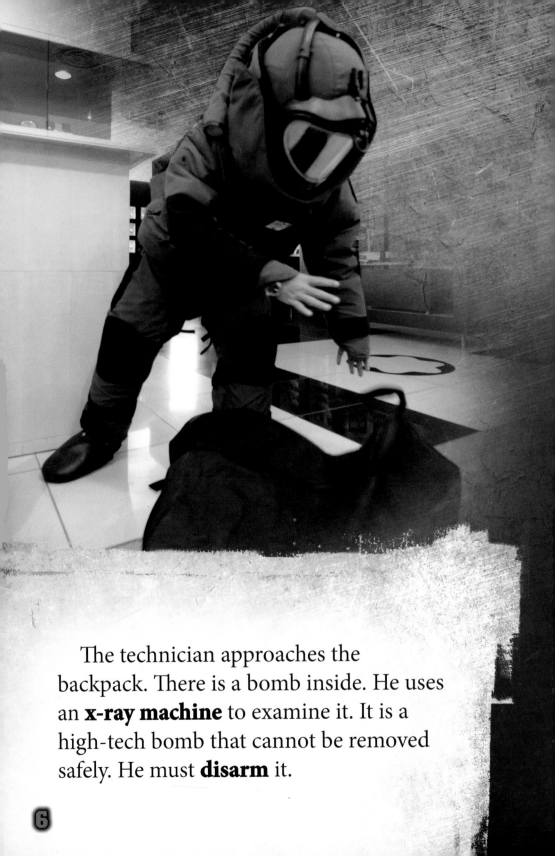

The technician approaches the backpack. There is a bomb inside. He uses an **x-ray machine** to examine it. It is a high-tech bomb that cannot be removed safely. He must **disarm** it.

The technician carefully drills a hole in the bomb. One wrong move and it will explode. He removes the **fuse**. Then he takes out the explosive material and puts it in a safe container. The bomb has been disarmed. Everyone is safe!

CHAPTER 2

BOMB SQUAD TECHNICIANS

Bomb squad technicians are highly trained professionals. Their job is to identify and disarm bombs and other **hazardous** devices. They can disarm anything from a homemade **pipe bomb** to a high-tech explosive. Technicians work for law enforcement or the military.

pipe bomb

An Elite Group

Technicians who disarm bombs in the military are often members of the Special Forces. These brave soldiers perform high-risk missions with little support.

Bomb squad technicians need to be explosives experts. They must attend a 6-week training course at the Hazardous Devices School in Alabama. The **Federal Bureau of Investigation (FBI)** and United States Army run this school. Technicians get hands-on practice in addition to classroom learning.

Explosive Disposal

Bomb squad technicians often have to dispose of fireworks and explosives used during construction.

The Nose Knows

Many bomb squads use dogs to sniff out explosives and find hidden bombs.

Technicians study the electronics used in bombs. They learn which types of bombs are safe to move. Instructors show them how to safely **detonate** bombs. Technicians also learn how to gather **evidence** to help catch bomb makers.

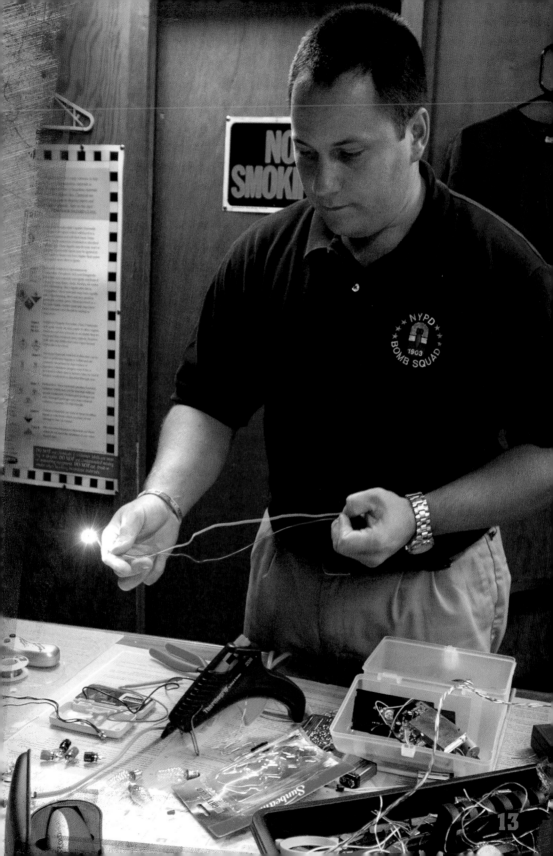

NO SMOKING

NYPD
★ ★
BOMB SQUAD
1903

Bomb squad technicians need a lot of gear. Protective suits keep them safe from accidental detonations. Robots with cameras help them examine explosives. Some robots can even disarm certain bombs. They carry **pigsticks** that shoot water to destroy a bomb's electronics.

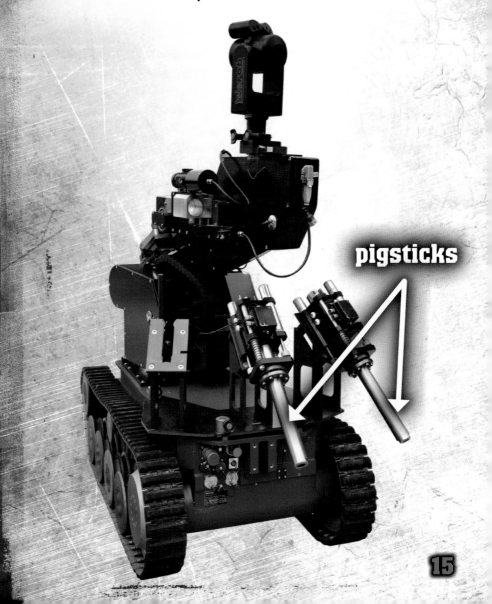

pigsticks

CHAPTER 3
DANGER!

Bomb squad technicians have high-stress, high-risk jobs. Protective suits cannot offer complete safety. **Shrapnel** can pierce the suits. Powerful bombs can even blast through the suits.

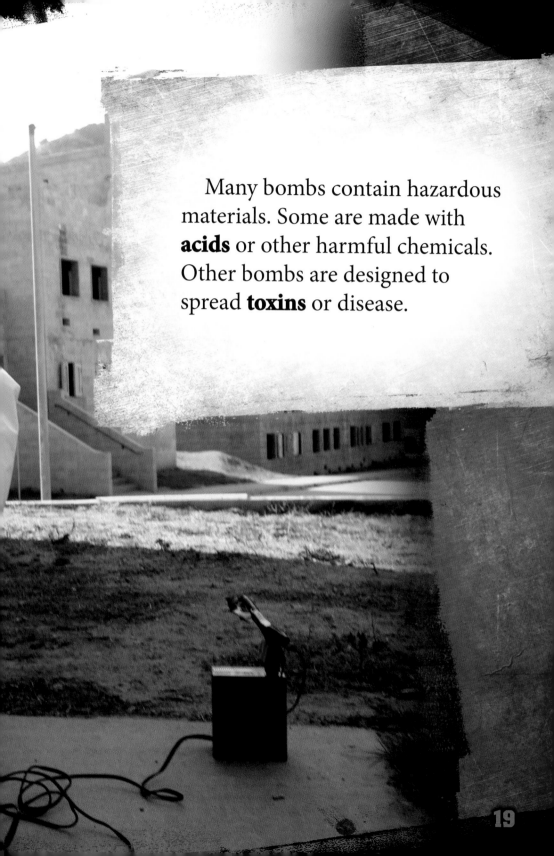

Many bombs contain hazardous materials. Some are made with **acids** or other harmful chemicals. Other bombs are designed to spread **toxins** or disease.

Nerves of Steel

A 2011 survey found that Americans believe bomb squad technicians have the scariest job.

Bomb squad technicians understand the dangers of their work. They use their skills and knowledge to safely disarm or destroy bombs. Technicians know they risk their lives every time they work with a bomb. They also know that their work saves lives.

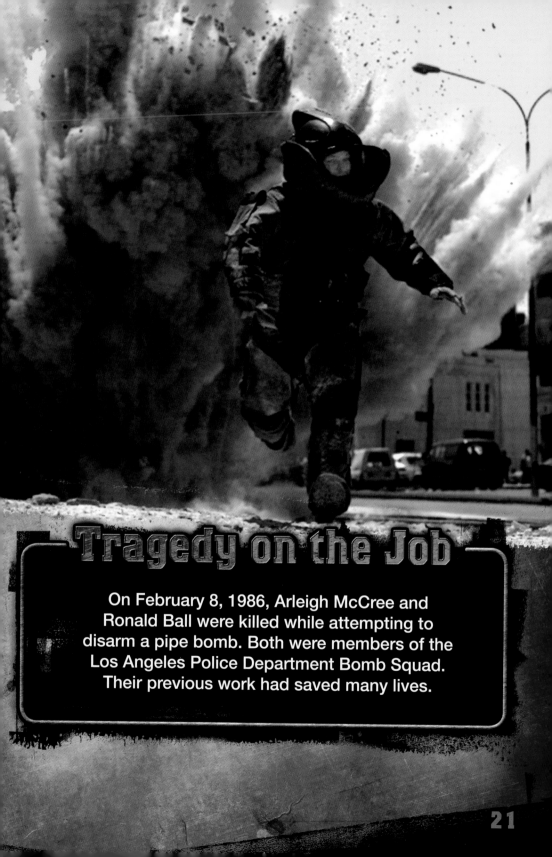

Tragedy on the Job

On February 8, 1986, Arleigh McCree and Ronald Ball were killed while attempting to disarm a pipe bomb. Both were members of the Los Angeles Police Department Bomb Squad. Their previous work had saved many lives.

Glossary

acids—liquids that can cause severe burns

detonate—to cause a bomb to explode

disarm—to take away the destructive power of a weapon

evacuate—to clear out of an area; people evacuate places where bombs have been found.

evidence—facts or information that support a conclusion or explanation

Federal Bureau of Investigation (FBI)—a government agency that investigates federal crimes

fuse—the part of a bomb that sets off the explosive material

hazardous—involving risk of harm or loss

pigsticks—tools that shoot powerful streams of water to disarm a bomb

pipe bomb—a pipe filled with explosive material

shrapnel—jagged bits of metal that fly out at high speeds during an explosion

toxins—substances that are poisonous to living beings

x-ray machine—a machine that uses x-ray technology to see inside objects; x-rays are powerful waves of energy that can go through solid objects.

To Learn More

AT THE LIBRARY

Gonzalez, Lissette. *Bomb Squads in Action*. New York, N.Y.:
PowerKids Press: Rosen, 2008.

Murdico, Suzanne J. *Bomb Squad Experts: Life Defusing
Explosive Devices*. New York, N.Y.: Rosen Pub. Group, 2004.

Reeves, Diane Lindsey. *Scary Jobs*. New York, N.Y.: Ferguson,
2009.

ON THE WEB

Learning more about
bomb squad technicians is as easy as 1, 2, 3.

1. Go to www.factsurfer.com.

2. Enter "bomb squad technicians" into the search box.

3. Click the "Surf" button and you will see a list of
related Web sites.

With factsurfer.com, finding more information
is just a click away.

Index